THE LAND FLIPPER ON ROADS

E.B. FARMER

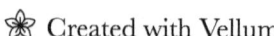

INTRODUCTION

One day, as a young man, I was agonizing out-loud about a problem. Agonizing out-loud is important. It makes you form your vague worries into real English words. It clarifies the problem and puts it out there into the world.

So a seller was offering 100 acres, but in two tracts and in different locations – a 60 out in the sticks and a 40 closer to civilization. The 60 was jam-packed with timber and way underpriced, a serious steal, but the 40 was just some regular nondescript tract, priced at just about its actual value.

My problem and the source of my angst? Well, he would only sell the two tracts together, as a package.

Oh, what to do, what to do! How can I talk the seller out of tying the two tracts together as a single sale?

"Don't," my dad answered. "Go ahead and buy them both and immediately sell the 40 back out again. Then you've got the 60 for the price you want to pay for it. You don't have to negotiate and you don't have to worry about someone else beating you to the deal. Just go ahead and give the seller what he wants."

Dad was a smart guy, really good at solving problems.

Anyway, I did that. I bought both tracts – the 60 with its tons and tons of timber after which I lusted, along with the plain-Jane 40 which I couldn't have cared less about.

And so that's how I came to own the 40. And there I was.

A couple of weeks later, as I mused on flipping the 40, I had an idea of my own. Along with my plan to buy timberland and reduce its cost with the sale of the standing timber, I'd also had thoughts of buying big cartons of Land Widgets and selling them out at retail. Parceling them out.

So this is my opportunity. I own this forty acres and want to sell it. So why not try to sell it in smaller tracts? Like 10-acre tracts? Why not take this chance to see if l can do a crude land-development deal?

Problem: The 40 had almost no road frontage – just a small public road which dead-ended at its corner. If I sold it in 10-acre tracts, how would those owners access their plots of land?

Hmm. I guess I'll have to build a road.

If you've read our earlier books, or if you just happen to know about rural land, you know that the #1 feature of a rural tract, at least so far as maximizing its value, is road frontage. That's what the landflipper is always hunting... a tract with long road frontage so you can chop it into smaller pieces.

But what if you can't find such a tract?

Well, in some cases, you can create such a tract yourself.

The 40 was worth about $40,000, which is what I had paid for it. But after building my $8,000 road − actually just a wide driveway − I sold the four 10-acre tracts for $100,000. And quickly.

So I made $52,000 in about four months. Dad was proud.

Don't read this book and expect to come out on the other side ready to build a subdivision. I couldn't teach you that even if I wanted. No one can. It's too complex, too local. I can't even teach you how to build your road.

But I can introduce you to the concept of road-building... the one thing you can do to vastly increase the value of your tract of rural land.

So let's talk roads.

Disclaimer: Road-building is a local endeavor and you will need local experts to advise you with any specific road project you undertake. We are not professionals in the field of road-building. This book is just a review of some of our experiences with and personal opinions about building roads. So don't rely on information from this book to guide your own project. Consult local experts.

CHAPTER 1

CONCEIVING YOUR ROAD

WHAT'S A ROAD? Well, I'd say it's some stretch of cleared ground on which you can travel with a wheeled vehicle.

But that could be the same as a 'trail', couldn't it? I've seen four-wheeler trails snaking through dense forest. Around this tree, between those trees, through that mudhole.

No, I think a road must be such a stretch of cleared ground which has somehow been 'prepared' or 'constructed'.

Yeah. A road – unlike a trail – has to be built by humans.

So imagine that you set your mind to building a piece of furniture. You'd have to do some planning. What kind of wood or other material? What will this furniture be used for? What kind of tools will I need to build it?

Same with a road, of course.

Here are a few of the questions you'll need to ask before

beginning to build a road into your tract of land, either for your own ease of access or with the idea of eventually selling off parcels of your land to be accessed by your new road:

What kind of traffic?

Four-wheelers? Eighteen-wheelers? Regular cars?

Big difference. I've seen loaded dump trucks sink six inches into a road which wasn't meant to hold weight like that. I've also seen roads so narrow that even a large pickup truck couldn't maneuver on them.

How wide will the ROW (right of way) be?

The ROW is the strip of land within which the road is built, and its width can be critical, especially if you ever want to turn your road over to the public (town or county).

You don't deed 'the road' to the county, of course. You deed the ROW to the county.

Along with the actual road – the raised, prepared surface – your ROW contains the road ditches, which we'll cover later as one of the most critical elements of road-building. The ROW also usually contains some or all of the utility lines. Power, water, gas, telephone... they will generally run along the outer ditch banks or even be buried deep beneath the bottom of the road ditch.

So, especially if you think your road will ever be owned by a government and used by the public, you need to research (ask the country and/or town) and think hard about the width of the ROW.

60-feet wide is 'normal' for a regular, residential road right of way. There are reasons for that, which I'll discuss later.

Specialized Hint: Regarding power poles, you should be closely involved in their locations. The power company will send out a truck with a large auger and some poles. Be there. Make them set their poles on the outer edge of the ROW, 12 inches in front of your lot-corner pipes. Don't let them drill exactly over the corner, uprooting the surveyor's pipe. Not unless you want an angry, cursing, bill-inflating surveyor. Be there for the pole-setting operation.

Where, exactly, will the ROW be located?

One time I decided to build a road across a field and into some woods. There was a drain perpendicular to my road, and the land narrowed as it approached the woods. So I really wasn't sure just where my road should run. I mean, it had to go through the approximate center of my land, but I wanted the best aesthetics I could get.

So I went out early one morning and I drove my truck where I thought the road should go. I did that three times and then chose the set of double tire tracks – outlined in the dewy field grass – which I liked best. Then I pin-flagged my ROW based on those.

After I constructed the road, Mr. Surveyor shot (located) its centerline and drew its ROW on our maps, thirty feet each way, perpendicular to the road's center.

Other times, you might help the surveyor draw your ROW on the plat, have him flag it out across your field and woods, and then build your road within his flags... according to plan.

Is this an all-weather road?

Unless it's for four-wheelers only, it had better be suitable for wet-weather traffic.

If it's a road through the Rockies or the desert, you might not need to worry much about how you'll top it, but if it's a regular road across regular dirt, you should think about the topping before you even begin. The type of topping – gravel, asphalt, other types of aggregate, concrete – may inform decisions about earlier construction work.

Who is going to maintain this road?

There's no problem with this issue if your road is used only by you and yours, but you should be thinking into the future. When two different interests or entities begin using the same road, the question of maintenance becomes critical, as detailed later, and as related to the last item, below.

Access: Who can use the road and who can't?

This is the big one. So big that I'm putting it here at the end, so we can segue into a whole chapter about it.

The answer to this question has ramifications in all sorts of directions – from maintenance to gating to actual life and death.

Vague, unclear access situations have led to some of the most vicious bitch fights I've ever encountered in the land business.

CHAPTER 2

PRIVATE, PUBLIC OR QUASI-PUBLIC?

Legal Use

ONE TIME I owned a tract of land and decided to build a road into it, but because of the overall configuration, the only place I could build the first stretch of road was along my property line.

So I called my neighbor: "Hey, do you want to throw in with me, share the construction cost, and have a bunch of new road frontage along your property line?"

"No," he answered.

So I drew my ROW five feet off of his property line, parallel to his fence, and I built my road there, leaving five feet of private property between my ROW and his land.

A couple of years later, his son came out, tossed a culvert in my road ditch and prepared to build a driveway onto his father's land.

I called the cops.

In the end, he picked up his culvert and went away, banned from ever even driving on my road again, much less trying to use it to access his dad's land.

It was my road. Actually, by that time, it belonged to the homeowner's association which I had created, and so it was what I call a "quasi-public" road. The only people who could use it were the lot owners back there – the members of the homeowners' association (HOA) and their invitees. I'll briefly discuss PUDs and HOAs a little later. For now, bear with me as I tell you more stories like the one above. It's so important – this issue of exactly who can and can't use your road.

I once contracted to buy a piece of land which had tons of road frontage, but much of that frontage was on a private road. A week later, I had to let the deal go when that private-road-owning neighbor absolutely refused to negotiate usage. He was angry that I'd even *called* him about it. I still remember the tension in his voice – the short, hard breaths between each of his curt responses.

One of the more tragic stories regarding this issue can be found by searching for *'neighbor montana murder gate'* or something like that. Read about how Landowner Campbell, in 2013, gunned down Neighbor Newman over a road-use disagreement.

There can be some crazy-intense emotion with this issue.

And it's rarely clear-cut, even from the law's viewpoint.

I once built a road with a cul-de-sac. The neighboring

landowner, a genuine donkey's ass, insisted that he should be able to drive from the end of my cul-de-sac into his property behind it.

But that would mean crossing over my cul-de-sac lots, lessening their aesthetic and monetary value. It might also mean lots more traffic through the neighborhood – which I had probably promised to my lotbuyers as a quiet cul-de-sac with no through traffic. So that would be another blow to its value, not to mention making me look like a dishonest real estate guy.

So the ass's ass appealed to the county, to whom I had deeded the road, but they declined involvement. Then he threatened to sue everyone. In the end, he made me confront him physically – when I caught him clearing the land between my cul-de-sac and his property. His face blanched as he stepped down from his tractor and noticed my open carry. He was startled and upset by it, even though he was aggressing against me. He was trespassing on my private property after I'd repeatedly warned him to stay off, tearing down vegetation on my two private lots, along with trying to bully me.

So, clearly, the ass had a different view of things than I did. Or than the county did. Who knows what a judge's outlook might've been. Thankfully, we never had to find out.

Sometimes it's hard to tell the good guys from the bad guys in a situation like this. As I say, even the courts can struggle with it. There's the issue of historical use, for example. Adverse possession. Prescriptive easements. Grandfathering. And even more complex laws. I remember once trying to buy a tract in a neighboring state. The lawyer told me that I might be able to force access across a neighbor and I might not. It depended on whether any of my predecessors in title had ever caused the property to be landlocked by selling off some or all of its frontage. Even a hundred years ago or more. Did he want me to research the particulars regarding this tract – at $175 per hour? He'd have to find old maps, see where roads had been located in 1890 and forward, research all ownerships and start contacting great grandnephews and the ex-wives of great uncles, and....

I walked away, of course.

In the Montana case, I understand that the neighbors had used that road for years to access a national forest. Then some guy (Campbell) bought the land under the road and put up a locked gate.

Then Neighbor Newman cut his locks.

Then Landowner Campbell... well... bullets.

Think hard about your road, whether it will be private, quasi-private or public. Try to avoid, upfront, the possibility of judges and hot lead and prison time, if at all possible.

Be clear about all of that from the start.

Maintenance

Along with the access issue is the maintenance issue. Who pays for it? Who has the right to come onto the road with a construction crew? Who has the obligation to do that? (Usually the guy at the end of the road.)

If you live at the end of a non-governmentally-maintained or non-HOA-maintained road, what do you do if an up-front neighbor lets loggers in during the winter, making the road usable only by airboat, and then refuses to even talk about fixing it? Maybe he lives out of state and doesn't care a thing about that road or maybe he lives on the corner of the blacktop and the private gravel road. What does he care if the gravel road falls apart?

Meanwhile, your whole life is on stop. Full stop. You can't even drive to your home anymore.

I've encountered several cases where the guy at the end of a private, unpaved road owns a tractor and a leveling blade. He's gotta.

I've also been involved in crafting legal agreements between neighbors regarding maintenance. It's like people who live on a dammed lake. What happens if the dam breaks? Well, we hope that the lakeside residents have a shared-use-and-maintenance agreement. Otherwise, they now all have frontage on a mud flat rather than on a beautiful lake, and they need to find a volunteer hero to come and fix it.

By the way, for the landflipper there is an upside to this issue. If you are looking to buy a tract of land on a private road, you can dangle a carrot. Tell the neighbors that you will spend some money on the road and also handle getting an agreement drawn up for the future, so they won't have to spend their weekends shoveling gravel out of wheelbarrows and into potholes anymore. Grab the situation and civilize things.

They'll love you for it and will be readier to tolerate the new neighbors whom you bring in when you sell tracts at the end of the road.

Can You Sell Tracts Off of It?

Such a question... the answer to which could mean the difference between wealth and impoverishment.

When my dad was newly-married, he went outside of a major city and bought a five-acre lot. But he chose one of the five-acre lots with a ROW next to it, running down its long side. I don't know if he did that on purpose or exactly how it came about, but an extra 60 feet of property separated us from the neighbor on that side. I remember as a kid, the neighbor and my dad would sometimes raise gardens on it.

Fast forward 20 years and there is my dad, mired in serious financial trouble because of certain uncontrollable issues... but saved by his new lots. A developer, to access a large tract behind Dad's property, had come in and turned that old ROW into a concrete, curb-and-gutter, residential street.

And there sat my dad, with eight very desirable and very valuable lots running down the length of his five-acre tract.

The difference between being able to sell a bunch of lots and NOT being able to do so? Well, that can sometimes be a life-changing difference.

Right now I know of a 20-acre tract at the end of a

private road. It's a road with individuals living on it, toward the back, across the private road from his land. The guy is trying to sell his 20 acres back there for $100,000, but with no takers, which is strange. Broken into four or five residential lots, that 20 acres is worth maybe $350,000.

The problem? Well, the folks on that private road have a very bad attitude. They don't want new neighbors. One of them, up on the corner of the blacktop, has planted an exotic tree right next to the gravel road surface, on the road side of the ditch. It's so close that a big lumber truck could never turn off the blacktop and into that road without destroying the tree. (Much less could a single-wide mobile home be pulled in there.)

So there sits a quarter of a million dollars, frozen, unable to be placed into the owner's wallet − not without a long and expensive legal fight with an uncertain outcome.

But even without the neighbor issue, could you legally sell lots off of that existing private road? Well, that depends on the county or town rules. I know of one county with a rule that you CAN sell lots off a private road, but only a maximum of six and only if the private road has been in continual use for at least eight years. Something like that.

So study the fine print of the county and/or town rules regarding roads before you start to build − even if your road will be private − and think hard about the legal status of your ROW.

HINT: Find a connected lawyer to help in situations like this. His or her aunt might sit on the planning board. Even if no one will give you a special favor, you will have the inside track on the rules for private road usage. And to keep those legal fees coming in, the lawyer and his aunt may be inclined to brainstorm for some kind of legal workaround – to make your project work.

CHAPTER 3

PLANNING YOUR ROAD

FIRST, remember that I'm talking about rural driveways up to asphalt residential roads, with open ditches. If you're building anything more sophisticated than that, for example a concrete-surfaced road or a curb-and-guttered road, you'll need a lot more than this book, even just as a primer or overview.

Dirt Guys

So you've decided to build a driveway/rural road.

But you're a smart person, so your first step is NOT a leap up onto the bulldozer to start pushing trees down and dirt around, all willy-nilly. No, you're going to start by planning your road's exact location, the width of its ROW, its actual width on the ground, its composition, the placement of its culverts and all such as that.

Spend a buck on road planning... save twenty on road building.

So. Do you need an engineer?

Depends. If it's going to be a public road, you'll likely be required to have an engineer overseeing it, stamping it with his formal approval.

Probably, but not always. Depends on the jurisdiction.

If an engineer is not required or even if one is required, my advice is to spend a lot of time hunting down – meeting and interviewing – an experienced dirt man. A contractor who deals with moving dirt and other material around.

Many times over the years I accompanied my dirt guy, walking the length of the proposed road, each of us with a tablet and pen in one hand and a laser level rod in the other, making notes, drawing, shooting elevations, studying topo maps, talking it over. Sometimes we'd come upon a spot which would make a nice pond, or an area to put some of the overburden which we muck out of the roadway.

We studied it out, talked it out, and made an overall plan.

In order to get the job, a good dirt guy has to involve himself in all the planning. He will insist on doing the planning himself or else studying and approving plans made by others. And his planning is often or usually free.

Remember that the difference between one dirt guy and the next is the same difference you'll find between all of your contacts, between all humans. Some are slow-witted, lazy, uninterested. Others are highly-competent and maybe even masterful. A good dirt guy is better than a mediocre engineer and sometimes as good as the best engineer, at least so far as smallish road-building goes. He's been involved in the actual work. He knows how things are likely to turn out, especially in his local area, with its local soils, local aggregate suppliers, local truckers, etc.

As with anyone you ever hire, try to go see his previous work. Talk to former clients. Especially in the case of road-building, you should out and go look at roads he built years ago. The test of a road is its durability.

Awhile back, we were clearing some land with a new dirt contractor, and the differences were brought home for me. The new guy started digging a burn pit 150 back from the public road, in exactly the spot where a homeowner would want to place his house, rather than digging it up near the road, between the setback line and the road, where buildings would be prohibited by our deed restrictions. Later, I instructed him to leave a tree every 75 feet in a certain area, but he took all of them down. I think maybe he just liked pushing trees down and didn't think it was a big deal, to follow my instructions.

My old dirt guy buddy, now retired, would never have done that. He was always thinking ahead and imagining the future, along with its potential problems. And he knew me – that I was finicky, almost a perfectionist. He'd never take a tree down to which I had extended a reprieve or pardon. Sometimes I walked along as he worked, giving a thumbs-up or thumbs-down to this tree and that one.

Find a good dirt contractor and imagine the future with him.

Get some free planning advice out of him while you're at it.

CAUTION: You should **never** walk anywhere in the vicinity of these big machines without a bright, preferably-fluorescent shirt and hat. And as you walk, watch the operator. Make eye contact with him before you move. Be sure he knows where you are. And if the machines are logging, stay even further away. One time I was safely away from a tree cutter, but he cut a tree which then landed on a dead tree which then crashed down toward me, landing within only a couple of feet. Be wary and be nimble.

EXTRA HINT: Large trees are your friends. Stand behind one as you watch the action. If he's a good operator, he'll stay away from those, so as not to damage the roots. If there are no trees, stand behind some sacred object which an operator would never disturb. A vehicle, a stack of supplies, whatever.

Imagining the Future

A few years ago, a distant cousin called me asking for advice. Some timber company had contacted him about accessing their plantation through his land. They were offering to pay him money AND build the road across his land, back to their timber. He wanted to know what I thought.

"Well, you should make them build it exactly where you want it – probably through the center of your land, for possible later development – and make them use a standard ROW width, which is usually 60 feet, even if you get a little less cash from them."

"But their road will only be about 10 feet wide," he said.

"That's OK. While they've got all that heavy equipment out there, make them build a standard roadbed, with good sloped ditches and concrete culverts, and exactly where it will do you the most good. Then they can only lay rock ten feet wide on top of the roadbed. Years from now, all you've got to do is widen out that rock to about 22 feet, maybe cover it with asphalt, and you're done. You won't even have to do much compacting, since those loaded log trucks will have pounded it down for so long."

He ignored me, letting them build a 10-foot-wide driveway, poorly ditched, along his property fenceline. Utterly useless to his heirs should they ever want or need to sell lots. If he'd done what I suggested, they might have one day saved tens of thousands of dollars, along with months or even years of time between themselves and their riches.

Hey. Shortsighted distant cousins. Whatchagonnado.

Even if you are building a glorified driveway into your property, think about future lot layouts. Find out the minimum road frontage and lot size required by your jurisdiction. Shoot (have the surveyor locate) the drains. Plan to use them as future lot lines.

Imagine your lots... even if you have no plans of ever selling lots. Just setting it up that way will make your land more valuable.

ROW Details

Residential road ROWs are usually 60 feet wide for a reason, as I mentioned.

Start with the approximate width of vehicles.

Regular car = 7.0 feet.

Big truck = 8.5 feet.

So you're going to need at least 17 feet of road width if you want two eighteen-wheelers to be able to scrape past each other.

But we'll be generous. Let's give them 20 feet of width, on the hard surface, plus an extra foot or two of improved (graveled) road shoulder on either side of the driving surface.

All of this presumes that you will now or later turn this into a residential street. If you're sure it will always be a driveway, you can make the hard surface as narrow as 8-10 feet. Or, as I suggested to my (very) distant and (very) idiot cousin, you could consider building the roadbed to residential width and only laying rock 8- to 10-feet wide on the surface.

So anyway, we've got a 20-foot-wide hard (gravel or asphalt) road surface with a couple of feet on either side for when you're drunk and just don't care enough about holding the road anymore.

Which makes the road bed – the raised hill of dirt running from here to yonder – about 24 feet wide.

OK.

So.

A road bed 24 feet wide.

But we've got a 60-foot-wide ROW.

So that leaves 18 feet on either side of our roadbed – between the roadbed and the edge of our ROW.

What do we do with that extra width?

Ditches

My dirt guy buddy was once waxing talkative about how much he hated water. "I don't want it anywhere near my road," he said. "Actually, to tell the truth, I'd like to pass an ordinance and ban it from anywhere in this entire neighborhood." He looked up. "Matter of fact, I'm pissed about it being up there in those clouds. It's too close!"

Yeah, dirt guys hate water. That's because roads hate it. Water will destroy a road faster than anything – even a horde of brats on dirt bikes.

And so we build ditches all alongside our roadbed, usually on both sides, to run that water off to the nearest creek or drain. Sometimes we have to run the ditches underneath our roads, usually with culverts, maybe even with a bridge. Whatever it takes, we work to divert the water away from our raised roadbed.

On gravel roads, watch other drivers. The ones who splash roughly through puddles? Those guys either don't know a thing about the destructive power of water or else they're probably some kind of criminals.

Probably. I'm just saying.

But the cars which tiptoe around the puddles? Those drivers are experienced with water and roads. They've watched those puddles grow with each pounding and splashing, sometimes even making the road impassible.

They probably live at the end of that road, those puddle tiptoers.

So back to our ROW.

We'd got an 18-foot-wide strip of land on either side of our roadbed, and we're going to build a ditch along it.

The thing is... ditch banks need to be mowed. So you can't just get out there with a backhoe and dig a trench on either side of your road, although that is certainly done in some places and some times. Better, though, is to slope downward toward the bottom of your ditch and then slope back up again to the edge of your ROW. A gentle slope, gentle enough to mow. About 9 feet down and 9 feet back up, using up that extra 18 feet of ROW on either side of your roadbed.

So that's why you need a 60-foot ROW for residential streets.

20' for the traffic.

4' for the shoulders. (2' on either side.)

36' for the ditches. (18' on either side.)

Approximately. Usually. Mosttimes. Check with your dirt guy, with your terrain, and with your local government.

By the way, sometimes you'll be walking through the

woods and you'll come upon depressed, sunken old road-ways, often along a section line. Those are either ancient horse-and-wagon roads or else, more likely, used for logging. The reason they are sunken, rather than raised, is that they are only good for dry-weather travel. They're useless when wet.

Loggers don't work timber in wet weather because their machines are too heavy for it. So they build dry-weather roads back into the timber tract by scraping down to the hard, supportive clay and pushing all the overburden to the sides. That overburden is made up of leaves, sticks and the soft soil which has been created over the years by their decomposition. So you'll often see ridges along the sides of these sunken roads, even with 100-year-old trees growing along those ridges.

Cul-de-Sacs

If your road is going to dead end, give a little planning thought to your cul-de-sac (aka: turnaround). Find some subdivision plats online and see how you can save a bunch of road-building money by playing a cul-de-sac in the right way. Check with your local government. Usually there will be special, reduced frontage requirements for cul-de-sac lots.

I once encountered a county with a fairly elaborate formula for deciding cul-de-sac lot frontages. A certain percentage of lots could have reduced frontage, etc.

Road building is a big deal. Expensive and time consuming.

Plan ahead.

Tying to Public Roads

One more thing to keep in mind is exactly where your road will tie into a public road. Go there. Crouch, as if driving a small car, and look both directions. Is there a sharp curve? A hilltop? Imagine yourself accelerating out of your new road onto the public highway. No problem? Or problem? Remember that accelerating out of a gravel driveway or road may requires a little more time than from a hard-surfaced road, especially if your gravel is loose.

You should also get into your car or truck and approach your new road entrance from both directions. Any problems?

I have a friend whose house I'm nervous about leaving. It is impossibly dangerous to back out of his driveway. You have to exit going forward, and you have to watch the hilltop to your left and speed out of his driveway while nervously studying your rearview mirror for any vehicles topping the hill behind you and bearing down on you.

If you can adjust your road entrance to a better spot, try to do that.

There is even a chance that the local government won't let you place your entrance there, so be sure you are good with all permitting, especially a permit for the culvert under your road entrance where it meets a public road.

CHAPTER 4

ROUGHING-IN YOUR ROAD

Equipment

SOMEBODY'S GOTTA bring some big old Boy Toys to this party.

Dirt's heavy. I remember the first time I saw a road grader work, up close. It parted that dirt like a spatula knifing through cake dough, like a carpenter's plane shaving off a thick curl of wood.

OK, lousy metaphors. I guess you've just got to see it for yourself. These machines have huge blades and buckets, powerful engines, cleats on all their shoes and hydraulic power which can crush a bowling ball as casually as an over-ripe tomato.

Keeping in mind that terminology will vary from place to place, here's a quick overview:

Bulldozer: It only has a front blade, but the thing can

move in three ways. Up and down. Left side forward, right side forward. Left side up, right side up. They have cleated tracks, like you might see on a military tank, because all they do is push heavy loads of dirt or other material. Modern ones have finger controls, like playing a video game. An enclosed, air conditioned cab is normal except on the smallest ones. Because of their cleated tracks, they can't be driven on a hard-surfaced road. If you have land on both sides of the road, the operator will either have to lay plywood to drive across or else load his monster up on the trailer and drive it across.

Hoe: Think of a hoe as a bucket on a human arm. It has a shoulder, an upside down elbow, and a wrist. Plus, it's sitting in a swivel chair, so it can spin and roll side to side and forward and back. A **trackhoe** has a really big digging bucket and tracks which may not be cleated. It doesn't need cleats since 1) it's lifting heavy loads rather than pushing them and 2) its hydraulic arm can pull itself out of any situation. To see how these arms can do most anything, search for "*backhoe loading itself into a truck*" and watch a video. A **backhoe** usually has rubber tires, a hoe on one end, and a loader bucket on the other end. The operator can turn his seat and controls to face either direction. These machines can be used for pushing down trees, reaching up high and using the tree's own weight against it. No tree has a chance. (And if it does, the hoe will cut its roots on all sides and then push again.) Sometimes they have a 'thumb' on their bucket and can be used to pick up heavy logs and other debris and load it into trucks. Even without a thumb, it can load lots of dirt into lots of dump trucks. But a hoe's main job, by far, is digging holes. Maybe you need to burn some trees. Things burn better in holes, where the heat radiates back to the burning material. Maybe you need to mine some clay or dig a pond. Get yourself a hoe.

Dump Truck: Many sizes. Small ones are sometimes called bobtails, meaning they don't have detachable trailers. They might carry 6-12 cubic yards of material. Big ones, tractor-trailers, might haul 24 yards or more. A cubic yard is a block of dirt 36 inches tall, 36 wide, and 36 deep. Sometimes your dirt guy will have his own dump trucks. Sometimes he'll hire them as needed for your job.

Grader: aka: **motor patrol grader**, **motor grader.** This machine is for shaping up your roadbed after you've got it roughly like you want it. (Dozers usually do the rough shaping.) The grader has a long blade hanging underneath the machine. Graders are also used for shaping and repairing – maintaining – gravel roads.

Scraper: aka: **tractor scraper.** A self-propelled tractor or pulled implement which scrapes up dirt into a hopper and takes it elsewhere to dump. Since it is wheeled, it's a lot faster than a dozer for moving dirt.

Tractor: A handy tool when road-building. You need a front-end loader, and you can attach various dirt-working implements on the back.

Skid Steer: aka: **skid loader, skid-steer loader**. Some people call them **Bobcats**, I'm guessing because the Bobcat Company made the first ones? It's a smallish, usually-tracked-but-sometimes-wheeled machine which can be equipped with a whole bunch of specialized attachments. Search online and see the variety of jobs these things can do, from mulching its way through a forest to digging post holes to....

Water truck: A truck with a big tank which sprinkles water on your road bed when it's too dry. You can't shape or compact dust. You've got to make it doughy first.

Sheepsfoot: Like a steamroller except with spikes which compress the soil. It can be self-propelled or just an implement to drag behind a tractor or dozer.

There are lots of other machines out there. Your dirt

guy will surely have some gadget which I haven't mentioned here... to make the job easier, faster, better.

Marking the ROW Corridor

As I said earlier, you can either build your road wherever you want it, visually, or else you can draw it on your plat first and then build it where the drawing demands it to be. If you build it by eye, walk the length of it, flagging the centerline as you go. Then send the dozer though. Then check how it looks and adjust. When you've got it in the right place, pull half the ROW distance each direction from the centerline and mark that. You do this with flagged or spray-painted lathes (wooden stakes) every 50-150 feet or so, outlining your work area or ROW corridor. In an open field, you can use pinflags instead of lathes.

If you choose the second technique, drawing your ROW on paper first, the surveyor will need to set the ROW stakes for you.

TIP: One good way to judge a machine operator's ability is to watch how he treats your lathes. If he runs over them or disrespects them in other ways, start looking for a new guy. An attentive operator will treat your lathes and pinflags as if they are the toes of (his own) small children.

Clearing the ROW

So it's time for your first big job -- clearing the ROW. Do this entirely, from edge to edge. You are going to need that space for ditching, utilities, etc. Remember, too that saving a large tree right on the edge of your corridor might not work out anyway, considering that many of its roots may be cut or damaged during construction. Even if it survives, it may send those roots out again to maybe interfere with the mowability of your ditch slopes.

If your land is wooded, you could have it timbered first, but then you'll have to hoe out all of your stumps – a considerable expense. If you leave the trees whole, they're a lot easier to knock over, to uproot. See if you can locate a small-time timber guy in the area. He might come in and take the logs for you as the dozer or hoe lays them down. If you don't timber it first, just let your dozer and/or hoe rampage through there, laying everything on the ground. Make sure the operators have got the ground drainable while you wait 2-4 weeks for all that green vegetation to get into the mood to burn.

Begin thinking about erosion control at this stage. You can do this with those black cloth silt fences or with temporary or permanent catch basins downstream from your work. These are basically just holes to catch the runoff and allow the dirt to settle out of it before the water continues draining off your land. Sometimes you can even do it with debris, blocking the runoff drains with piles of downed trees and brush. Such permeable barriers slow the water long enough for the dirt to settle out of it.

Anyway, just imagine yourself as a downstream neighbor. Do you want new soil washed down onto your property? You might or might not, but it's best to assume that your neighbor doesn't.

So far as disposing of the downed vegetation in your corridor, I won't go into detail on that. You and your dirt guy need to talk it out. Maybe he'll dig a pit or two for burning. Maybe he'll let firewood guys go in and lighten the burn piles. Maybe he'll put everything into dump trucks and haul it away. If you burn and you're in a hurry, consider renting one of those huge fans which can reduce the greatest stump to a charcoal briquet in no time at all.

HINT: Since the dozer will be in there anyway, pushing and burning, consider having him brush the land on either side of your road and burning that, too. Even if it's a private driveway, it's nice to have a park-like setting to ride through rather than just two walls of woods. Plus, that smaller brush will help get your fires started and hot.

Also, think carefully about the location of any pit you decide to dig. Don't put one under your road, for example. That dirt needs to be highly compacted. Don't put one where a dwelling might ever be built, etc.

Leave a mound of dirt on top of the filled pit, to account for settling in the first couple of years.

Mucking Out the ROW

At the end of this first clearing stage, your ROW will still have roots and small debris and 'trash dirt' in it. It may also have the remains of your burn piles.

So now you need to muck all of that out – all the organic material and the soft, sandy, semi-organic dirt – with a dozer or hoe. Sometimes you can push it out of the ROW and lose it (fan and feather it out) on the natural ground. Sometimes you'll truck it away. You might even dig a pit, mine clay out of it for your road base, and fill the pit with that useless material.

When I say that it's useless, I mean useless for road building. It can be quite valuable later, as yard fill. Just ask any independent trucker. He'll tell you that every caller he gets for fill dirt will insist, "But I want topsoil!"

NOTE: They say not to cover tree roots with more than six inches of new dirt. Consult with someone if you're going to feather the mucked out topsoil into a set of woods.

· · ·

Rough Grading the Road

So now you've got a sort of depressed valley running from here to yonder – your cleared and mucked-out ROW corridor – and you've got to start building the raised roadbed and constructing the ditches. This is where the road begins to take shape as distinguishable from the raw land.

Depending on local conditions, the dozer might be able to take the material from the ditches, as it cuts them, and push that toward the center of the ROW to be used in making the roadbed. Also, there will be hills and valleys along your cleared corridor. Some of that material will be cut and some will be filled. Your dirt guy or engineer will study it and make decisions about dirt movement.

Once you're got the ditches roughed in and the beginnings of a long loaf of dirt running between them, you'll have to work the sub-base. Often the dozer can just mix the natural sandy soil with the clay soil for that. A masterful dirt guy will have left just the right amount of sand for the job. During this operation, you'll probably need a sheepsfoot or other soil-compacting machine. The dozer lays down a six-inch lift (layer of soil) and the sheepsfoot compacts it. They work together.

If your road is mostly just a driveway, you might kinda-sorta skip the sheepsfooting step. The dozer itself could compact your sub-base well enough if you'll just have light traffic. But keep in mind that it could settle unevenly, forcing you to come back later and reshape it.

HINT: At this stage, with the rough roadbed in place, you should do any utility trenching across it. I have driven on rough country roads where the roadbuilder waited until he had a finished road before thinking to trench across it with utility lines. Very bad idea. Trench early. Let the roadbed be settling before you do your finish work or add your toppings.

Also, as you are forming up the roadbed, you'll have to deal with drainage. You need an overall plan to get the water away from your roadbed, ASAP.

Ditches and Culverts

Have you seen roads which run through narrow valleys? They always run alongside the stream or river, which is functioning as the ditch on that downhill side. Paralleling the road on the uphill side is usually a road ditch whose contents, every now and again, will need to cross the road and be dumped into the river. For that, we'll need a culvert under our road.

Even if you and your dirt guy are building this road yourself, you may need an engineer at this point, to tell you what size and type of culvert. Sometimes the federal government might size your culverts for you. I can't remember for sure, but try contacting the NRCS or somebody about that. [*NRCS = Natural Resources Conservation Service, formerly known as the Soil Conservation Service, an agency of the United States Department of Agriculture that provides technical assistance to farmers and other private landowners and managers.*]

Often the county or town or state will insist on sizing the culvert for you as part of a permitting process, especially where your road ties in to a public road or, of course, if your road will be public.

But even so, this is a good chance to educate yourself about the concept of the "watershed" – also sometimes known as a "drainage basin" or "catchment".

The watershed is that area of land which catches rainwater and drains it toward and through your road culvert. If you've got ten acres of flat pasture land draining through your culvert, that's a whole lot different than 200 acres of steep parking-lot land, and the two situations will require very different culverts.

For fun and for your education, get a topo map and draw your new road and culverts on it. Then sit and study it, imagining that you are a drop of rainwater. If you fall in this spot, will you eventually run through that new culvert being installed under that new road? Draw a line separating the land upon which raindrops WILL flow through the culvert, as opposed to those raindrops which will flow in a different direction. Mostly you'll be outlining the local ridges. When you finish, you'll have a crude drawing of your culvert's watershed – often a semi-circle or maybe just a blob – whose acreage you can determine.

So far as culvert types, if you can get away with corrugated plastic, I'd go with that. Galvanized metal, even if tar-coated, will rust away more quickly, so I'm told. Concrete is great and very permanent, but what a damned chore. Culverts have to be set at the correct elevation and they have to be tilted so that water will flow out of them rather than collecting in a pool inside them. When you've got six-

or eight-foot sections of heavy concrete to line up like that, it's way harder than a single 30- or 40-foot length of corrugated plastic, trust me. The internet says that the corrugated plastic may last in excess of 100 years. That's good enough for me.

Remember that if you get the culvert size wrong and install one which is too small, you can usually add another one alongside it. But also remember that two 12-inch culverts will not carry as much as one 24-inch culvert. It's more like a factor of four, I think. (But I am not a professional geometrist, so ask your engineer about that.)

So go big, is my suggestion. Even if your road doesn't breach from a too-small culvert, rainwater will gush out of an undersized culvert with such force that it may scour out a hole on the downhill side, which hole may then hold water on a permanent basis.

So go big. What the heck.

Consider rip rap (large stones) protection on both ends, to slow the water as it approaches and leaves your culvert.

If you've got a really, really big body of water wanting to cross your road, you can buy a railroad tanker car with both ends cut off and use that. They are advertised in some of the construction mags. I myself would not consider building a bridge, except as an extreme last resort, and only if it were used on private land. That's a big-time engineering and construction project.

CHAPTER 5

FINISHING YOUR ROAD

Final Roadbed Grading

SO NOW YOU'VE roughed-in a raised, highly-compacted roadbed, properly ditched and culverted. If this is just a driveway, you're almost finished. You just need to shape it up with a motor grader or even just a tractor-pulled scraper blade and add some aggregate – some rock.

Consider doing both projects at once – the final shaping and the rock-laying – especially if you've hired a grader. Those things are expensive. As the grader is finishing up with the shaping, get the dump trucks rolling in, dumping their piles. The grader does a fine job of spreading aggregate.

And by the way, be sure that your grader operator is an expert because among other things, he needs to carefully 'crown' your road. Roads are all about shedding water. So water that falls in the center of your road shouldn't just stand around. Instead, it needs to immediately start running for the exits (the ditches).

So your road will be slightly crowned by the grader operator, at least on the straightaways. If you lay a long pole across it, the pole should balance on the centerpoint – while out at the edges you should see daylight between the pole and the road surface.

SURFACING YOUR ROAD

Aggregates

So much depends on what sort of road you are building, but aggregates will come into play no matter what. Aggregates are small bits of hard stuff, aggregated into large quantities. Sand and gravel, for example. Sand is, I guess, the smallest aggregate used in construction. If you go smaller, you're into dust or 'fines', which can still be useful, as I'll mention further along.

The largest aggregate? I dunno... rip rap, maybe? For those who don't know, rip rap is rock so big that even a rugged guy like me couldn't play toss-and-catch with the larger chunks. (Kidding. I could barely even pick up some of the larger chunks.) Rip rap is used as shoring on sloped ground, mostly, or as a surface to catch and slow rushing water.

With roads, aggregate can be used as the final topping,

as with a gravel road, but it's also used underneath hard-surfaced roads. The base or sub-base needs to be rock-strong.

If you are building a driveway, you might just lay the aggregate 2"-3" thick, assuming you are starting with a well-compacted dirt base and you don't drive an 18-wheeler for a career or as a hobby.

If it's going to be a gravel road, 5" − 8" of gravel on top of the compacted dirt base might be enough, although more is better.

If a residential asphalt road, maybe 6" − 8" under the final asphalt. Again, more is better. Talk it out with your engineer and dirt guy.

Read the internet and talk to your construction guys about specific types of aggregates, especially about what is available in the local area.

Meanwhile, I'll mention a few here in passing.

Crushed stone. They've got huge stone-crushing machines somewhere. Up in the mountains, I guess. I've never seen one, but I understand there are screens of differing sizes which catch and sort the material as it falls through from the crushing. Rip rap gets trapped in the first screen, then smaller stones (maybe for landscaping work?) and so forth, all the way down to about two inch rocks.

Unlike river gravel, crushed rock has angled shoulders. With the smaller stuff, down around two inches, these angular rocks mix and lock together with the fines − the dust from the crushing – to make a great support or base layer for traffic. This material is all sorted and graded. I've heard the 2" rock, with fines, called *SB2*, or *sub-base, 2-inch maximum*. But read about those grades and uses online if you're interested. They crush all sorts of rock, from granite to limestone.

Crushed Concrete. Yeah, they collect broken concrete, remove the rebar somehow, and run it through the crusher. It makes a fine heavy-duty base. And because so much of aggregate cost comes from the shipping, crushed concrete could be a better choice if you live far from the mountains or other rock source. You can also get crushed asphalt, which I understand might melt down with the heat and make an impermeable driveway surface.

Washed gravel. There are a bunch of driveways and country roads topped with this stuff. It has rounded shoulders but will mix in with the fines and set up pretty hard most of the time. I would guess that you'll need more of it to make the same strength as a crushed rock surface, but I could be exactly wrong about that.

Miscellaneous: Anything hard and small can be used. Collect your marbles until they fill a dump truck bed. Slag rock, left over from smelting operations. Railroad ballast, used sometimes because it drains well. Near the coasts, they even use clam shells and oyster shells as driveway material. Ask around in your area.

NOTE: About asking around in your area, I once knew a guy who was building a road in an area where state contractors were working to grind and remove the old asphalt surface from a state highway before laying new hot mix. They approached the guy and asked if he wanted to buy it, which he did. They both got a deal. The contractors got a place to dump it nearby, for some money, and the guy got a cheap material for his roadbed. Keep your eyes open for opportunity.

NOTE: The 2" crushed rock, with fines, can actually be laid with an asphalt laydown machine. Doing that, rather than using a grader to spread it 1) gets the depth exactly right and 2) lays it in an undisturbed bed, with the fines and rock well-mixed and 3) lays it exactly the right width, keeping it all right there in the middle for you.

Asphalt

Asphalt is thick tarry stuff which occurs naturally or else is refined from oil. The Brits call it bitumen. You've heard of asphalt singles. The stuff is waterproof and sticky.

The proper term for the mixture of asphalt and fine aggregate, used for road topping, is actually 'asphalt concrete' but Americans usually just call it asphalt.

'Hot mix' is a another term you'll hear for it. There will be a local asphalt plant which heats the asphalt, mixes it with the aggregate (tiny stuff, like maybe pea gravel) and loads it into dump trucks, which must deliver the stuff within a particular time window or else it might harden in their truck beds. When these trucks arrive on site, they dump the mix into an asphalt-laying machine which then applies it a certain depth and width on your road. These machines don't spread it much more than 10-feet wide, so they will usually lay two ribbons of it on a residential road... to make the total 20 feet of hard surface.

The machines may lay it slightly tilted, by the way, in

order to preserve the road crown which we discussed earlier. If the crown is already there, in the base surface, I guess they just lay asphalt on top of that contour.

Two or three inches of thickness will usually be enough for a residential road. But you have to have built a stiff base, since asphalt has no real strength. If your base fails, your asphalt will fail. Also, keep in mind that if you want two inches of asphalt, you'll have to lay 2.5 or 3 three inches. That's because as the asphalt is laid down, a roller machine will track back and forth across it, compacting it, squeezing out the air.

By the way, laying asphalt is a loud and hot and chaotic experience, with trucks and rollers and laydown machines and men walking everywhere with shovels and special rakes. It's best to stand back and watch from a distance. A friend of mine, an asphalt contractor, told me a story about one of his workers. When a truck began to back up, this guy didn't distinguish its *beepbeepbeep* from the other noises and activities around him, and he was crushed.

Be careful out there.

Concrete

If you are building a concrete road, you'll need to look elsewhere, even for the sort of informal and rudimentary information which I'm trying to convey here. It's a whole nother piece of business from driveways and rural roads, and I've never been involved in one's construction. The good news (I think) is that your base can be a little iffier, since concrete does indeed have its own strength. That's what I've heard, anyway.

Curbs and gutters? Same deal. I've only ever worked with open-ditch roads, although I have observed the construction of concrete, curb-and-gutter roads.

CHAPTER 6

FINAL TOUCHES AND MISCELLANEOUS NOTES

SO YOU'VE BUILT a fine gravel or asphalt road, either for your own use or for selling off tracts and getting rich.

During the first week after completion, you are legally allowed to go out each day and stand on a hilltop and just admire it. You can even send ditch pics to your friends or to strangers, along with long explanations of their culvert sizes, their slopes and lengths. Whatever.

But once you've gotten over your admirations and your braggings, it's time for the finish-up work.

Signs

Even if the road or oversized driveway will only be used by your family, consider signs.

I suggest **zebra signs** to warn of culvert drop offs and other spots where extra caution may be needed. One sign facing traffic might be OK, but you could put two, one on either side of the road. I would consider putting them roughly 30-50 feet before the risky area, but use your own judgment along with guidance from the internet or your local government authority.

How about a **street sign** where your road connects to the public roadway? I've seen those which simply read: *Jones Family Road*. Friends looking for your house will find it helpful. So will utility guys and pizza guys and deputies responding to an emergency. Also, believe it or not, there's a chance that a cheap roadname sign could help legitimize your road. If you or your heirs ever petition the county to take your road into its system, the road's legitimacy may be partially judged based on whether it is or is not a 'named road'. Think about 'named waterways' and how critical that term can become in some legal situations.

So consider making a name for your road and putting up a sign. (Just don't name it after one of my pets. That's been done to death.)

Also think about a **STOP** sign**,** even if it's a long, private, oversized driveway. Everyone knows that you're supposed to stop where your driveway makes a 'T' with the public road, right? But maybe go ahead and install the STOP sign anyway. It'll make you feel better. Some kid, just learning to drive, might need a reminder. Maybe a distracted driver leaving your home could use an extra bit of bright red warning. Read online or in your county regs about how big your signs should be, how high, how placed.

This is also the time to consider a **Private Road** sign. You might even have one made for the occasion which says: **Do Not Enter This Road** (or **Drive**) **Without Invitation By Owner**.

You can make signs to say most anything you want. They are pretty cheap and can make the world easier to understand and to maneuver.

.   .   .

Checkdams

But now let's turn to your biggest and most important post-road-construction project.

Which is making sure that your new road is protected from the elements.

Which means... protected from a road's greatest enemy.

Which means... water.

Just like everything else, water gathers momentum as it runs downhill. And water, unlike a sled or tractor tire, also gains volume as it goes. The longer it runs, the bigger and faster it gets. So long runs, especially in steep ditches, should be interrupted or 'checked' now and again. You can do that with rip rap or any chunks of material. The ditch water slows and pools at these checkdams before moving on. I will sometimes pound a couple of stakes in the ditch bottom, toss some debris uphill of it, and let the rushing water wash the debris down and catch at the stakes. You can also use hay bales.

Running water has so much energy that it can scour out your ditches with a single rain. So get your checkdams in place. Then you can move on to the final but absolutely necessary job of your whole project.

Grass

You've disturbed a lot of dirt. You've created bare slopes where there were no slopes before. These slopes will let rain-water have its easy way with them unless you do something to stop that. In the old days, I used to work in various ways to stop rainwater from degrading my work, but now I believe there's really no better option than planting grass. Its network of roots will keep your dirt in place like nothing else can.

Different grassing methods exist. You can lay mesh mats or erosion control blankets like they do on big-money jobs or small boutique jobs. I think those are probably used in conjunction with planted grass. They hold the soil in place until the seeds can grow.

There is also hydroseeding. A big tanker truck will come and spray a gluey substance on your slopes and road ditches. The glue contains grass seeds and fertilizer, and it is almost instantaneous protection. I understand that within an hour or so, rain won't dislodge it, and within 4-6 weeks, you'll have lush fields of grass everywhere that got the glue.

Then there's just a guy spreading grass seed himself. If you have a tractor, you can buy an implement for that, a seed spreader. Or you can hire someone to do it. The tractor implement will be a big hopper which you'll fill it with grass seed and fertilizer. Your PTO will operate the spreader.

Check with your local farmer's coop. They sometimes rent out grass-seeding hoppers, which are self-contained trailers to pull behind a tractor or truck. By some kind of gearwork, the wheels run the broadcasting mechanism. As you roll along, it casts a spray behind and several feet to either side of your trailer/hopper. With some of them, you can adjust the spray to go in only one direction.

If it's the right time of year, you can put in a fast-growing species like winter rye, mixed with a warm weather grass like Bermuda. The rye will jump up quickly and mostly hold the Bermuda seed in place until spring. Go to your farmer's coop or other rural hardware store and talk grass seeds and grass planting with those guys.

But you've got to do it — to get grass on those slopes. You've spent all that time and money, so protect your investment.

GENERAL NOTES:

Weather

If you are a road-builder or other guy who works with dirt, you will necessarily become weather obsessed. I can't help myself anymore. If you bump into me on the street, you can ask me about the next week's weather, and I may be able to rattle it off in some detail — especially how much rain is expected. My weather awareness comes from dirt-moving machines being so freaking big, like timber-cutting machines. They're huge and heavy, and the people who work them are dependent on them for their daily bread. If rain shuts them down, they have trouble buying new shoes for their babies. For me, it's only a delay of completion, but that could have some pretty serious consequences, too.

So become familiar with the weather in your area... how it works, where the fronts come from, what's the dry season in your area, why it often rains on hot afternoons and such.

It's so easy these days. Thank the tech guys. In the old days, out on the job, we used to study the sky like some kind of spiritual earth folk, ruminating on the hue of the clouds and their particular shape, the taste of the wind on our tongues, all in an effort to discern the quality and quantity of the approaching storm.

Now we just glance at our weather radar apps.

The Ground Man

Large machines work by the hour, usually, and it's always a big number. So you have a vested interest in keeping the machine operator 1) working and 2) honest with his hours.

So you need to try and be there when he's working. Always, if you can.

But even so, that's not enough. The way it works on big, ongoing jobs is that the operator will charge you from the time he arrives and cranks up his machine to the time he shuts it down, less maybe 30 minutes for lunch. He doesn't carry a stopwatch with him and click it every time he climbs down to take a leak behind the blade. He doesn't click a stopwatch if a limb tangles in his hydraulic hose and he has to climb around to dislodge it.

He should, but he doesn't. I've don't think I've ever been able to get an operator to charge me only for machine hours. Some have promised to do so, under their breaths, but don't count on that actually happening. If you're dickish about it, you might force him to do that, but being dickish about things will get you screwed in other ways.

So what does all of this means?

It means you can make $150/hour, the same as the machine operator, if you hang around, ready to pull that limb out of his hydraulic hose or cut barbed wire out of his tracks so that he doesn't have to kill his machine and climb down and do it himself.

Nothing irritates me so much as watching a neighbor pull up at my job site and flag down the dozer operator for a chitchat. Nah. That's not going to happen. I'm not going to pay $150/hour for my operator to catch up on the latest gossip or explain exactly what's going on with this undertaking. I'll intercept the neighbor. I'll tell the operator that he is fired if he stops to talk to my neighbors.

Not only do you save money by doing all the ground work for the operator, but you make the job better and faster. You should try to imagine yourself as the operator. Is there an overhanging limb which interferes with his view of the job? Clip or saw it. Does it take the operator an extra 10 minutes to find his lunch bag before he starts eating it? Volunteer to go buy fast food, open it for him, lay it out on the tailgate. Is he running out of hydraulic fluid? Call your wife and have her bring out a 5-gallon can. Did a ROW lathe get knocked down? Fix it. Does the ROW need to be remeasured anywhere? Does the bottom of a culvert trench need some delicate shovel work?

Become the artist. Stand back and study the scene. Imagine yourself up on that machine, as the operator. Is there anything on the ground that can be adjusted, fixed, or moved in order to make the operator's job more efficient?

Do that stuff.

Best thing is to operate your tractor while he pushes dirt. You can save a bunch of money by moving a bit of dirt yourself, and you're always the one to climb down and handle some ground job like flagging off a pretty Dogwood tree or clipping the barbed wire before it gets tangled in his tracks.

Road Maintenance and Repair

Nothing lasts forever, but you can help your road live a longer and healthier life by keeping an eye on its ailments.

Sometimes, after a few months, the traffic will begin to show you the weak spots in your base. Watch for even the shallowest puddles in your asphalt surface after a rain. It's showing you the base weaknesses. If the puddles get worse and worse, you might have to dig out that spot with a hoe, fill it with crushed concrete, wait for the road traffic to compact that new material, and then get some fresh asphalt for that spot. There is something called 'cold mix' which you can apply yourself to small spots.

Then there is asphalt sealant. It's a tarry-oily substance which you pour along the cracks and then flatten out with a weird, V-shaped squeegee. You've doubtless seen the results of such an operation. The surface of the blacktop has a webwork of wide black lines. This stuff is important because – as we know – the enemy of all roads is water. If you don't fill those cracks, water seeps into the base, sometimes freezes, and your road gets a bad case of the crumbles.

. . .

A Word About PUDs

The issue of PUDs and HOAs deserves at least an entire chapter if not a whole book, but for the moment I'll only mention the most relevant aspect, as it relates to road-building.

PUD stands for **Planned Unit Development**. There are legal subtleties regarding different PUD configurations, but for now, whenever you hear me say PUD, just substitute **Condo Development**.

A PUD is a Condo Development.

HOA stands for **Homeowners' Association.**

Think about a condominium development. Such a development has real estate units (condos) which are owned by individuals. But in addition to the condos, the PUD has shared areas, usually called **Common Areas**. The common areas could include parking lots, a clubhouse, a pool, the grounds, the sidewalks, even roads.

These common areas are owned by the HOA, which is a legal entity. It's a corporation. Who owns the HOA? Well, the homeowners. Each condo owner is a voting member of the HOA. The HOA has officers, usually made up of condo owners.

So the condo owners own the HOA, which is an incorporated entity.

And the HOA owns the common areas.

So.

What do PUDs have to do with road construction?

Well, a road which belongs to a PUD is private. Think of it like the parking lots. Those are private. Think about a road leading back to a condo development. That road is private. So the governmental body with authority over the building of public roads generally, usually, maybe... doesn't have any control over how a condo development builds its parking lots. Nor its roads.

If your subdivision road is a common area of a PUD, then you may be able to build it however you like. Maybe your condo owners (five-acre tract buyers) are horse people and only want a gravel trail winding through their condo development (rural subdivision). It means you can maybe build whatever road you like, after organizing your rural subdivision as a PUD.

Just something to keep in the back of your mind. To ask your lawyer about if the occasion ever arises.

NOTE: If you want to gate your subdivision, you may be actually *required* to make it a PUD. Only if it's a private road can you gate the public out, although this issue is still being litigated in some places.

Cost

I'm sure you've noticed that I've given you no guidance at all regarding the cost, the dollars, of a road-building project. That is intentional. There's just no way that can be done. What if you have no trees? That could knock off a hundred hours of machine time or more. What if you're on rocky ground? Or a mud flat? What do dozers and hoes cost in your area?

Talk to contractors... a lot. In my view, you should educate yourself and run the numbers yourself. Think of this as your opportunity to really immerse yourself in this aspect of landflipping or land-owning. Become the expert. Even if you get lump-sum bids, work to understand the economics of the project. How much to clear? To grub? To rough-form and install culverts?

Road-building is hard and it's tricky, with problems coming out of the blue which need to be solved as cheaply as possible. Best to pay close attention through the whole process.

But it's pretty cool. And fun. And rewarding – an interesting experience which not many landowners have undertaken but which can increase the value of your land in aesthetic, practical and monetary ways.

Good luck with it.

www.ingramcontent.com/pod-product-compliance
Lightning Source LLC
Chambersburg PA
CBHW030524220526
45463CB00007B/2713